SCARFING BASICS

Cutting & Gluing,
Strong, Straight, & Clean
Scarf Joints
in
Plywood & Lumber

Written and photographed by
Russell Brown

Other Books by Russell Brown;

1. **EPOXY BASICS**, *WORKING WITH EPOXY CLEANLY & EFFICIENTLY*

2. **ROLLING PERFECTION**, *Roller Only Painting Method for Sprayed-look Finish Using Interlux® 2 part LP Paint*

Available in print and digital at PTWATERCRAFT.COM.
Also available on Amazon.com, and other outlets.

SCARFING BASICS; Cutting & Gluing, Strong, Straight, & Clean Scarf Joints in Plywood & Lumber, is a copyright product of Russell Brown and may not be reproduced in part or in full, without the written permission of the author.

Methods used in this book are those of the author and are not necessarily endorsed by companies whose products may be referenced here in. The author and his associates are not responsible for any injury or health issues that might occur as a result of working with these materials and tools. Please read all product information before use, and observe maximum shop saftey when working with epoxies, power tools, etc.

Russell and Ashlyn Brown started their kit boat business in 2009. Their company, Port Townsend Watercraft, aims to encourage the use of rowing/sailing tenders (especially nesting dinghies) as an alternative to motorized tenders, and fuel efficiency in motor boats. Learn more about their boat kits, and other products at www.ptwatercraft.com.

Thank you for purchasing this book!

Copyright Russell Brown September 2014
Edited by Ashlyn Brown
Published by Port Townsend Watercraft
www.ptwatercraft.com / info@ptwatercraft.com
Printed by CreateSpace online publishing

Cover background photo (plywood scarf) by James Curtis
Cover inset (lumber scarf) by Russell Brown
Cover design by Ashlyn Brown

TABLE OF CONTENTS

A Brief note from the editor 4

Part 1; Plywood

Cutting & Gluing, Strong, Straight, & Clean Scarf Joints 5
SCARF JOINT LAYOUT 6
CUTTING SCARF JOINTS 8
POSITIONING (ALIGNMENT) ..12
CLAMPING ..14
GLUING (plywood) ..15
    Gluing and Filler selection notes on pages 16 and 37 ..
SCARFING FULL 4FT WIDE PANELS ..19
MAKING SCARF JOINT PARALLEL TO SURFACE GRAIN ..19
FOR A POWER PLANER TO WORK WELL ..20
BUTT JOINTS IN PLYWOOD ..21

Part 2; Lumber

SCARFING LUMBER ..22
MAKING the TABLE SAW SLED JIG ..22
    -Marking for positioning ..25
TO MAKE A ROUTER JIG FOR WIDER PLANKS ..29
Gluing (lumber) ..35
NOTES ON SURFACE PREP, TEMP, AND GLUING. ..37
ADDENDUM: Filling holes with a syringe and color matching ..38

A brief note from the editor;

The following pages are full of text and photos. Topic headings are in blue and can be found at the top or down the page. As with Russell's boat building, efficient use of space is exercised in this book. In general, the more important the photo, the larger it is. Text sizes vary so don't worry about your eyes. When he could, he enlarged the text and made bold text to emphasize instructions.

It is also assumed in this book that the reader has epoxy skills. Otherwise, for accurately metering and thoroughly mixing epoxy, (plus many other useful tips) please see **EPOXY BASICS**, *WORKING WITH EPOXY CLEANLY & EFFICIENTLY, available in e-book(pdf) or print from Port Townsend Watercraft at ptwatercraft.com .*

Happy woodworking!
Ashlyn Brown

CUTTING AND GLUING STRONG , STRAIGHT, AND CLEAN SCARF JOINTS IN PLYWOOD

While a few methods exist for joining plywood panels, scarfing panels together is arguably the best. This is because a scarf can be as strong as the rest of the panel, as well as having a flat surface. It is also the most difficult method to do well.

Accurately cutting long joints in thin and floppy material is a big challenge. Gluing those long, thin, and floppy joints so that they come out flat, strong, and good looking is an even bigger challenge.

There are "easy ways" to scarf plywood, such as cutting them with an attachment on a skill saw and gluing them with buckets of nails or bricks to hold the joints flat, but the results are often poor.

A router jig can work well for cutting scarfs in lumber, but not for cutting long plywood scarfs. The skill saw attachment method can work okay on thinner plywood, but would be best used as a "roughing out" method after laying out the scarfs as shown on pages 6 & 7.

Gluing these long, flexible joints requires powerful and even clamping pressure.

I don't do scarfs "the easy way". I cut the joints by hand with a power planer and block plane. I use a very positive method for laying them out before cutting and also for clamping them when gluing. My scarfs come out flat, they look good and I'm often surprised how little time it takes.
Whether the reader agrees with all the methods shown or not, there will likely be techniques in this book that help make better scarf joints.

Doing good scarfs requires a flat table with sharp and straight edges.

The table shown here is merely a sheet of 3/4" particleboard with straight 2x4 framing screwed underneath, set on sawhorses. Even easier is to throw a new sheet of particle board on top of an existing flat table. Particle board (or MDF) is flat, cheap, and holds screws well.

SCARF JOINT LAYOUT

The important first step for cutting accurate scarf joints is cutting the panel edges (to be scarfed) *straight and square.*

Using the factory edge of the plywood is not recommended because not only is it usually dinged up and often not straight, but the sheet can be thinner at the ends from entering and exiting the factory sanding machine. *Thinner* means that it's the surface veneers that are thinner, not what you want near a scarf joint, so trim a bit off the ends of the panels where the scarfs will be.

If you have a Festool® skill saw and straightedge setup, this is easy. If not, a regular skill saw can be used against a clamped straightedge (straight wooden straightedge may work best).

Once trimmed, butt the parts together to check that they fit tight over the length of the joint and that the edges are square.

Arrange the parts to be joined on the table (9 mm thick cockpit seat tops shown). Identify (A-A, B-B, etc) **but more importantly, mark which side of each piece is to have the scarf cut.**
The larger piece (or middle piece if 3 pieces are being joined) should have the scarfs cut on the upper surface so that the larger (or middle) piece can stay on the table when gluing. The smaller, or end pieces should have the scarfs cut on their lower surfaces.
Scribble on these surfaces (in pencil) to insure cutting the scarf on the right face.

A crisp pencil line, the same distance back from the edge on both parts to be joined, is key to an accurate scarf joint.

Set your combination square tightly and use it as a scribe to mark an even distance back from the edges of both parts. Use a sharp pencil.

Scarf angle ratios are a debatable subject, but remember that the longer the scarf (10 or 12 : 1), the harder they are to cut.
We use 8 : 1 for plywood, so these scarfs in 9 mm (3/8") ply are about 3" wide.

CUTTING SCARF JOINTS

Clamp the piece being cut to the table with the edge flush with the table edge as shown below.

We use a power planer to remove the bulk of the material, setting it shallower and shallower as we approach the pencil line and face veneer.
This takes some skill, a decent power planer (see page 20), and a straight table edge.

A sharp jack plane or even a block plane can accomplish the same goal when scarfing thin plywood.

Often the angle of the cut needs to be modified as you are cutting This can be done by starting a new angle, making a pass with only half of the planer on the scarf and making another pass favoring the new angle, or for minor changes, just pushing down harder on one edge or the other.

Make full length passes with the planer generally.

Watch for evenly wide veneer layers.

Start the cut after the beginning and finish before the end (or whatever is needed) to keep the layers even.

Wind back on the blade depth knob early as you approach the goal.

NOTE:
Another way to "rough out" a scarf is with a skillsaw attachment made for cutting scarf joints.

While it is difficult to cut accurate joints with a skillsaw attachment, one could be used in conjunction with the layout method we show and finished by hand as described here.

If the planer is working well, one can cut pretty close to the final goal.

When cutting scarfs in thicker plywood the joint will likely be wider than the width of the planer. The planer will need to be held at an angle (as shown) and moved up or down the scarf. This effectively makes the bed as wide as you want so that the front end of the planer feels one edge of the scarf and the back end the other edge.

A nearly perfect scarf can be cut in a very short time by winding back on the cutting depth early and winding back some more (until just barely cutting) and always keeping the planer at an angle, IF you have a decent planer (page 20) with sharp blades.

To finish cutting the scarf, a really sharp block plane is the tool, but it must always be held at an angle to the cut (as shown) whether removing material from the edges or middle of the scarf.

The goal is to create a flat surface between the pencil line and the sharp "feather edge", but how sharp to make the feather edge? How sharp is your block plane? How crisp is the edge of your table? How good does the scarf joint need to look when finished?

We leave a bit of thickness to the edge for scarfs where a visible glue line is acceptable.
The inset below shows that when assembled, a reasonably sharp feather edge could still leave a 1/8" wide (or so) gap that will be filled when gluing. After block sanding the surfaces of the finished scarf, this visible line will be much narrower.

To make the feather edge sharper (without tearing) requires a very sharp plane and a straight and flat table edge.

A good guide when cutting is to keep the visible face of the feather edge veneer (far left in photo) a bit narrower than the veneer next to the pencil line.

The feather edge will be delicate regardless, but the sharper the edge, the more prone it is to being damaged before gluing.

Using the plane at an angle means that the ends of the plane feel the edges of the joint. The plane can be moved up or down to remove material from either edge, but when in the middle (as shown), the plane will remove humps and leave the joint very slightly hollow, which is fine.

Note that the edge of the scarf is flush with the edge of the table.

Check that there are no bumps over the length of the scarf as shown.

POSITIONING (ALIGNMENT)

When the scarfs are cut, clean the table and position the panels where they will be glued. Lock the larger panel (with scarf facing up) to the bench with a couple of nails before positioning the end panel(s). **See photo next page.**

Positioning the panels to be scarfed is a critical step.

The panels must be separated enough that a straightedge or combination square (shown) pressed down hard over the scarf shows a flat surface.

The first photo shows one panel trying to climb over the other. That's not good. The second photo shows the panels pulled away from each other enough to show a flat surface.

Check over the length of the scarf and re-position until a flat surface is achieved. **It's far better to have a thicker glue line than to have one panel trying to climb over the other** (that's what creates a lumpy scarf and sanding the lump away will thin the surface veneers).

The scarf joint in this photo is under the eraser. The larger panel (with scarf facing up) was nailed to the bench (arrows) before carefully positioning the end panel and nailing it to the bench.

These nails are critical for the alignment of panels when gluing. The nail holes can be filled when filling the screw holes. (we talk about screws on the next page)

The larger piece can be left nailed to the bench, but the end piece (or pieces) will be removed for glue application.

On the panel(s) to be removed, mark the bench along the edge of the panel, mark its position lengthwise (as shown on left), and **leave the nail tips protruding from the panel so that the panel can be quickly and positively re-located when gluing.**

CLAMPING

Unless you are scarfing very narrow panels and can clamp from both edges, the best way to achieve glue pressure when scarfing is with screws.

I know, screws leave screw holes and everyone wants to avoid that, but I ask, what's the big deal about holes? They are easy to fill (see page 18), one can color match so that they are almost invisible, and they are very necessary for scarfing plywood because **screws can provide clamping pressure where no normal clamp can reach.**

Screws combined with a "pressure plate" provide very even pressure over an area wider than the scarf. If the scarfs are positioned right and a pressure plate and screws are used, a flat scarf joint is virtually guaranteed.

Pressure plates should be at least 3/4" thick, whether made from plywood or particle board. The plate shown is 6" wide, twice the width of the scarf, with holes drilled 1" from the edges and spaced about 4" apart. Pressure plates can be used over and over again.

The screws used should be long enough to bite fully into (or through) the table.
More notes on screw pressure on page 19.
We used 2" long # 6 drywall type screws.

Drill holes in the pressure plate sized so that the screws can pass through easily.

The pressure plates should be centered over the scarf joint (with the joints aligned and the panels nailed to the bench).
In this case we measured out 1 1/2" from the edge of the joint (left side of photo) and aligned the edge of the plate to those marks.

Holes should be drilled through the panels being scarfed using the holes in the pressure plate as a guide.

If possible, clamp one edge of the pressure plate to hold it in place while drilling.

Choose a bit sized so that the screws being used can just pass through the hole.

Mark the bit with tape as shown to drill all the way through the panel being scarfed and into the bench about 1/16". Drilling into the bench slightly allows the screw to start without creating a bump that would hold the panel up off the bench.

Before removing the pressure plate, mark the length of one edge and identify as shown for easy re-positioning when gluing.

GLUING

Remove the end panels, but leave the nails poking through the panels for easy re-alignment.

Clean the bench well so the panels can lay flat when being glued.

Cut two pieces of plastic per scarf that are longer and more than twice as wide as the joint.

Slip plastic under the scarf joints as shown after checking that there's nothing caught under the scarfs that would keep them from laying flat.

Gluing starts with applying a coat of un-thickened epoxy to both surfaces. This is best done with a short piece of roller and a palette as shown. End grain plywood can soak up some epoxy, so be generous.

Unlike most glue joints, in a plywood scarf the excess glue has nowhere to go (except out the ends or onto the surface), so *excess thickened epoxy is to be avoided*. The fine teeth of a notched tooth spreader are perfect for metering out an even amount of epoxy *to one face of the joint only*.

Holding the spreader at a very flat angle (shown) will apply less thickened epoxy.

The epoxy should be thickened to a runny catsup consistency.

Fillers used for gluing:
About two thirds colloidal silica and one third micro fibers or high density fibers. (see pg 37 "Notes..")
(WEST SYSTEM® numbers respectively are: 406 Colloidal Silica, 403 Microfiber Filler, & 404 High Density Filler)

The rest is a breeze. The protruding nail tips should make re-alignment of the panels easy. Cover the joint with plastic as shown. Re-align the pressure plates and start all the screws before driving them hard into the bench.

It's best to tighten screws in the center first so that excess epoxy can start traveling out towards the ends of the joint.

Snug up on all the screws by hand after the glue has a chance to squeeze a bit.

Remove the pressure plate after an overnight cure. Ideally, the amount of squeezed out glue on the surface should look about like what's shown.

We like to fill all holes before block sanding the joint. Apply pieces of tape over each hole (rub down well), turn the panel over and inject each hole with a syringe.

The Addendum on Page 38 describes color matching using different fillers and methods for using syringes.

Sanding off the rock hard squeezed-out glue without dishing away the softer wood adjacent to the scarf is a challenge.
We use a fairly stiff 1/4" thick sanding block with 80 grit sandpaper. Taping the ends of the block as shown will keep the block cutting where it should, and not cutting where it shouldn't.

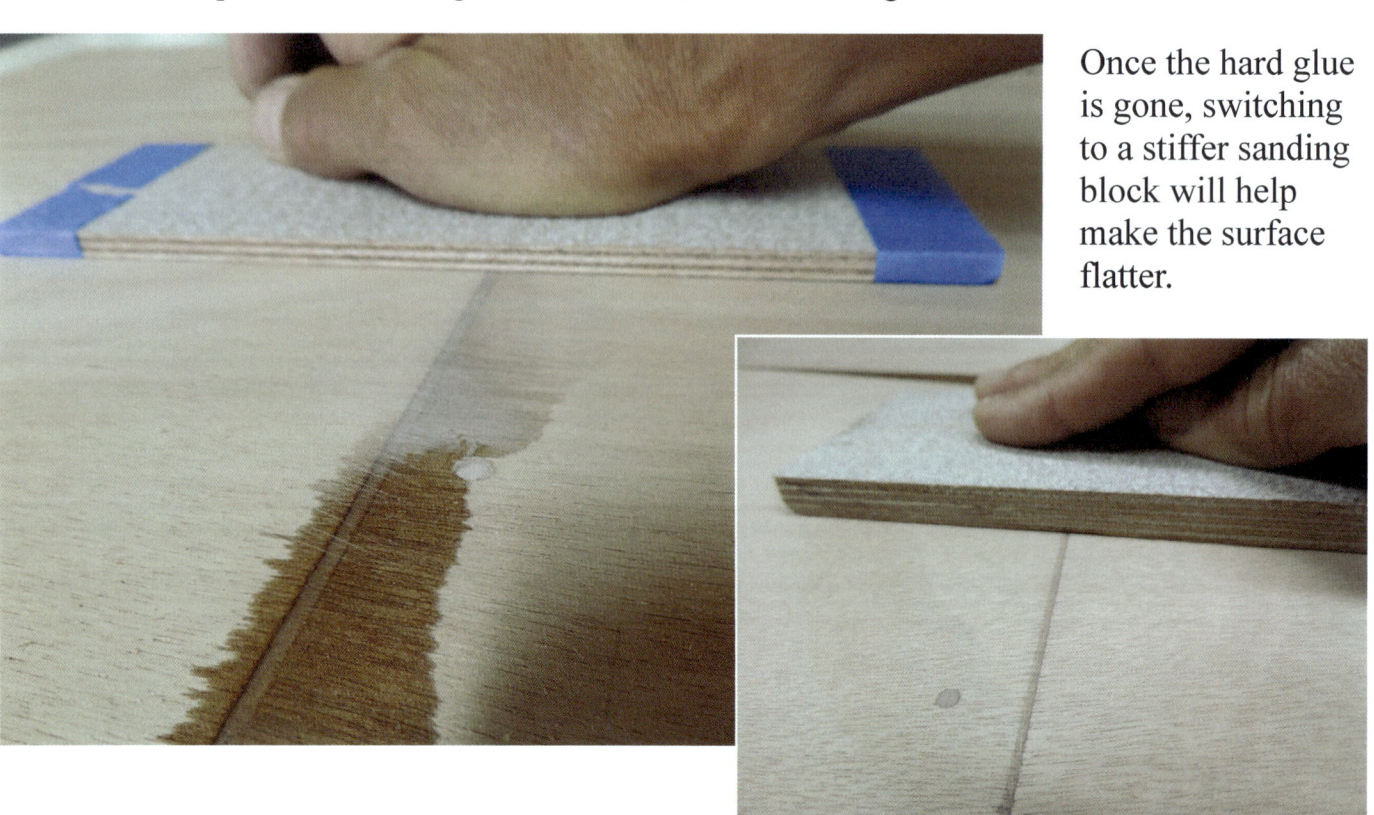

Once the hard glue is gone, switching to a stiffer sanding block will help make the surface flatter.

While it is easier to scarf narrower panels, **Scarfing Full 4 ft Wide Panels** is sometimes necessary. The photos below show a sample scarf being cut and glued.
Cutting these long scarfs is much easier if the end of the table is straight over its length.
Small waves in the table create bigger waves in the veneer layers as seen in photo on left.

Using screws that bite into the full thickness of the bench (or all the way through) is important.

This sample scarf was ruined as a result of mistakenly using shorter screws and having a few screws that stripped.

Besides not giving full pressure, stripping threads will actually hold the panel up off the surface of the bench.

Usually scarfs are done with the surface grain of the plywood at right angles to the scarf.
Making Scarf Joints Parallel to the Surface Grain is really challenging because the feather edge of the scarfs become extremely delicate.
There are times when this is necessary, such as when building bulkheads for larger boats. Sometimes these scarfs need to look good. For times like this, sharper tools, straighter table edges, and taking even more care are in order.

For a Power Planer to Work Well it must have three things that are easy to check for before you buy one. *The bed must be flat.* This is easy to check with a straightedge as shown. *The forward (adjustable) part of the bed must be on the same plane as the rest of the bed. Wind it level with the bed to check.* The planer shown came incredibly warped and bent, but it now has a cast epoxy base. That's another story...

The third important thing is blade depth.

Blade depth can be checked easily with a straight block or stick that is held flat to the main (back) bed of the planer. *The blades should be on the same plane or very slightly proud of the bed.*

Most planers now have disposable carbide blades that are pre-set for blade depth. That's all great if the blade depth is set correctly.

Butt joints in plywood can be surprisingly strong. Often strong enough to be able to assemble whatever is being built and later use fiberglass cloth on both sides to make the joint as strong as the rest of the plywood.

To make a butt joint strong, the most important thing is to generously prime both edges (short section of roller works best), then thicken the epoxy with gluing fillers and apply a small bead as shown to one edge. Both panels should be held on edge for epoxy application. One panel can then be nailed to the table over a strip of plastic packing tape (to avoid gluing the panels to the bench) before carefully placing the other panel and nailing.

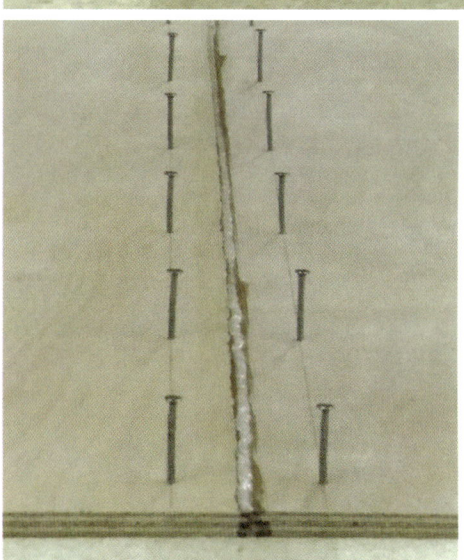

For thinner plywood, just pounding the nails partway into the table seems to work fine, but for thicker plywood it's best to use plywood pads. These are easy to break away with the sharp end of a hammer (when removing the nails) if they are cut about 1/2" x 1/2". Start the nails in the pads over a hole in the bench.

Nails should be close to the edges of the panels (3/4" or so). Still, tapping the edges flat as shown may be necessary.

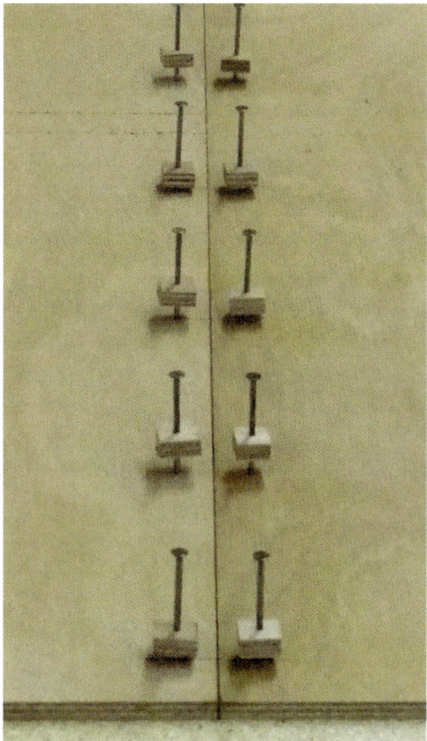

SCARFING LUMBER

Unlike scarfing plywood, there are easy ways to cut and glue scarfs in lumber, whether it's for hull stringers, scarfing planks for spar building, or just making short planks longer.

To cut scarfs easily requires jigs, one for the table saw and one for the router.

The table saw "sled" style jig is used for cutting stringer sized stock and can be used for wood up to about 2" in width depending on the size of your table saw.

The router jig, for cutting scarfs in wider planks, is a bit more of a project, but if you need the sled jig for scarfing smaller stock, build it first because the ramps for the router jig can be made on the table saw sled.

We chose a scarf ratio of 10 : 1 for both jigs.

Making the Table Saw Sled Jig requires a flat piece of plywood about 3/8" thick **and a stick that exactly fits the width of the channels that are cast into the table saw top.**
The stick should be milled (on the table saw) to fit the width of the channel without play, but also without much friction, so that it can slide but not wiggle. The stick can be cut to only about 2/3rds the depth of the channel (room for sawdust underneath).

Joining the plywood to the stick could be done with tiny screws. **We prefer to glue the two together while the stick is held straight in the channel.**

We cut some tiny pieces of squishy foam to push the stick up, syringed a small bead of 5 minute epoxy on the stick (not too much) and placed the plywood on top with lots of weight to push the stick back down flush with the surface (photo next page).

Wind the blade up and cut off the excess plywood as shown.

The last step is the only critical one:

The piece that stock will be clamped to (let's call it the fence) must be straight and square and *attached at the desired scarf angle, 10 : 1 in this case.*

We screw this piece from underneath with countersunk screws so that angles can be modified if needed.

Holding stock to the scarfing jig can be done with a clamp as shown, but **a stop is necessary to avoid the possibility of hitting the clamp with the saw blade.**

Serious injury could result from hitting a steel clamp with a carbide toothed blade.

With a longer table saw bed or when cutting thinner stock, a block can be clamped to the saw itself as a stop (*see next page*).

Here we used a piece of strong chord attached with a screw to the sled and tied to the saw as a stop.
The blade should exit the cut (and the sled hit the stop) a safe distance from the clamp.

Once a safe position is found for the clamp, mark the position on the fence, but this position will change depending on the thickness of the stock being scarfed.

When cutting thinner stock, a stop can be clamped to the saw as shown (far right of photo).

The resulting scarfs should be square at both ends and of equal lengths as shown below.

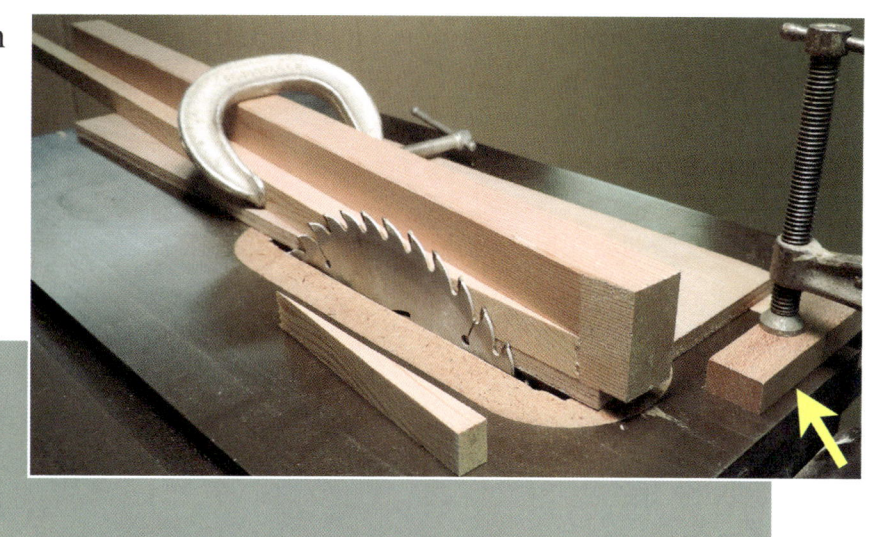

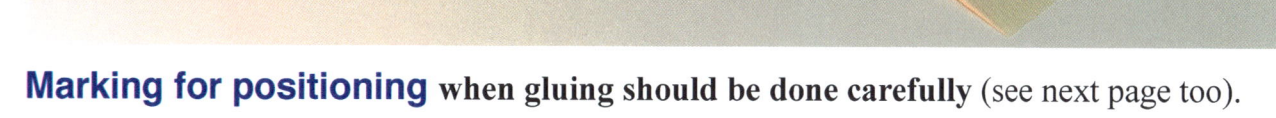

Marking for positioning when gluing should be done carefully (see next page too).

Sliding the scarfs toward each other on a flat surface with something straight above will show correct positioning. When moved too far toward each other, gaps will appear at either end.

When correctly positioned as below, mark as shown on next page.

Use a combination square and pencil to make marks for alignment when gluing.

A nice flat board is the perfect thing to glue scarfs on as it can be blocked up off the table to allow room for clamping.

A board that's not so nice and flat can be made so with a trip through a thickness planer.

To keep the parts straight edgeways when gluing, clamp something long and straight to one edge of the board.

The longer and straighter this piece is (let's call it a stop), the easier it will be to line the parts up when gluing.

You also may wish to use a "press" when gluing as shown on next page.

Gluing (please see notes page 16) starts with a thorough priming with un-thickened epoxy.

Apply more un-thickened epoxy after letting the first coat soak in for a bit.

Note the plastic sheeting applied to keep the parts from sticking to the board and stop.

Thicken a small amount of epoxy (see page 16 & 37 for filler selection) to catsup or mayonnaise consistency and **apply a small amount to one of the scarf faces** as shown on right.

Clamp the scarfs to the stop with the alignment marks lined up with each other. This should align the parts edgeways and keep the scarfs from sliding apart when clamping downward.

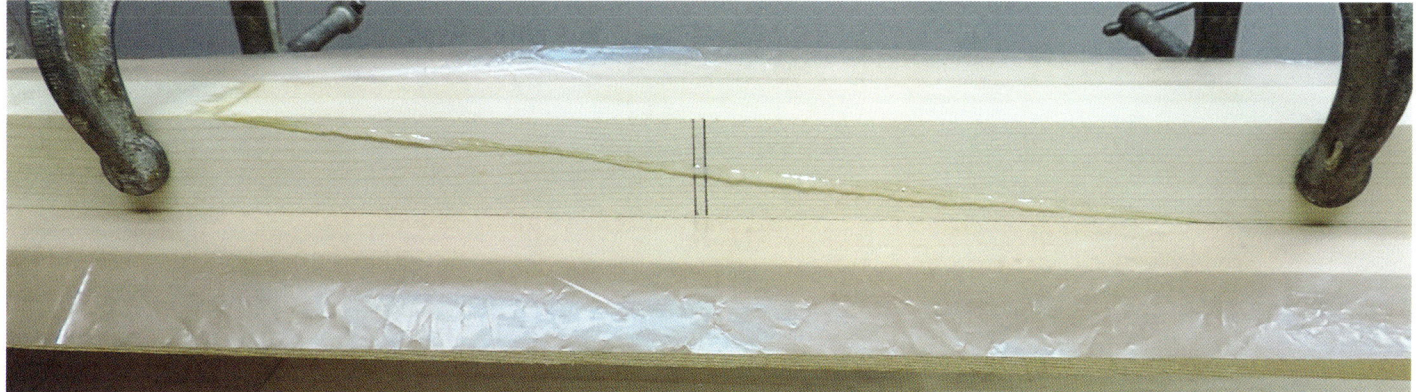

The "press" is simply a stiff and straight piece of wood used to apply even pressure over the length of the scarf. **We clamp only at either end of the scarf to avoid over-clamping** and the possibility of a "dry joint". Use sheet plastic under the press or apply plastic packing tape to it.

When gluing multiple scarf joints for parts such as hull stringers, jigs can be made where a scarf can be glued on either side.

These jigs can be blocked off the table, as shown, or they can rest on sawhorses.

Plastic packing tape was carefully applied to these jigs to make multiple uses easier, but plastic sheeting works fine too.

Taking the trouble to build jigs and use presses can really pay off. They make gluing easier and the resulting scarfs are reliably straight and clean.

We clean up the squeezed-out glue with a sharpened stick because it's always easier to clean up wet epoxy than it is to sand hard epoxy.

Blocking up the ends of the pieces being scarfed to the same level as the jig is necessary.

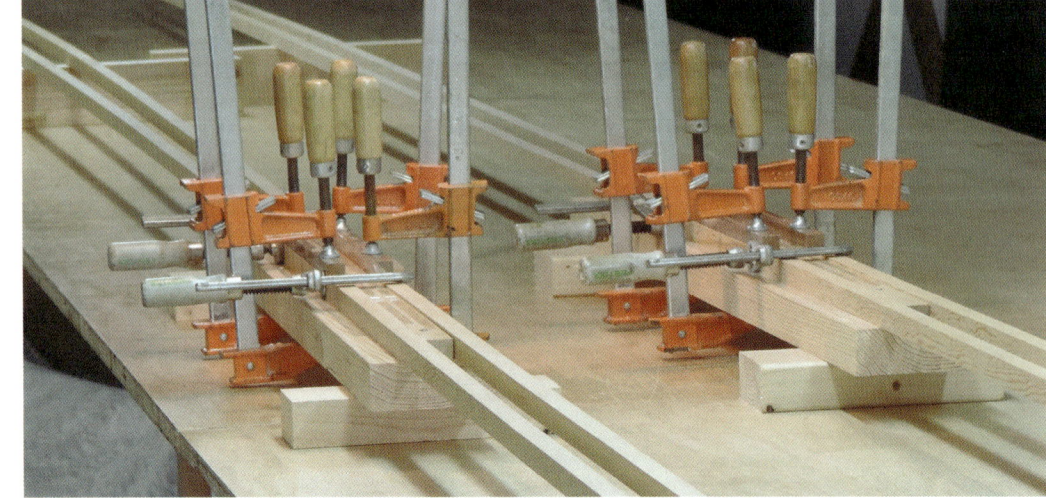

To Make a Router Jig for Scarfing Wider Planks

requires some flat & thick (3/4", at least) material. High quality plywood is best. Making the base from something really flat is the most important thing (see next page).

How long to make the jig depends on how thick the lumber being scarfed and the scarf angle.

The jig shown is for lumber up to 1 1/2" thick and a 10 : 1 scarf angle.

Because the ramps must be identical, we carefully cut (straight and square edges) two 2" x 20" pieces of 3/4" plywood and used the sled jig to cut them into the ramps.

To hold these parts to the sled jig, we screwed from underneath with two countersunk screws, the tips of which are visible below. The stock was clamped snugly to the fence before driving the screws.

Lay both ramps on something flat to check that they are identical.
Cut off the forward ends square while the two ramps are held together.

The base (shown below) should be longer than the ramps (in this case, 24") and about 2" wider than the widest stock being scarfed.
The base shown is 8" wide and will be used for scarfs up to 6" wide.

The ramps should be aligned fore & aft carefully. We cut the base with parallel edges and square ends and aligned the tips of the ramps with the front edge of the base.
Alignment nails (in pre-drilled, snug holes) make gluing the ramps on a breeze.

We used yellow glue (just because we could) and lots of clamps to insure that the ramps were tight and square to the base when glued.

The router needs a sled to slide up, down, and across the ramps. This sled is about 15" wide x 5", with a 2 1/2" diameter half-circle cut from one edge on center. 3/4" ply was used (must not bend).

The router base is screwed to the sled.

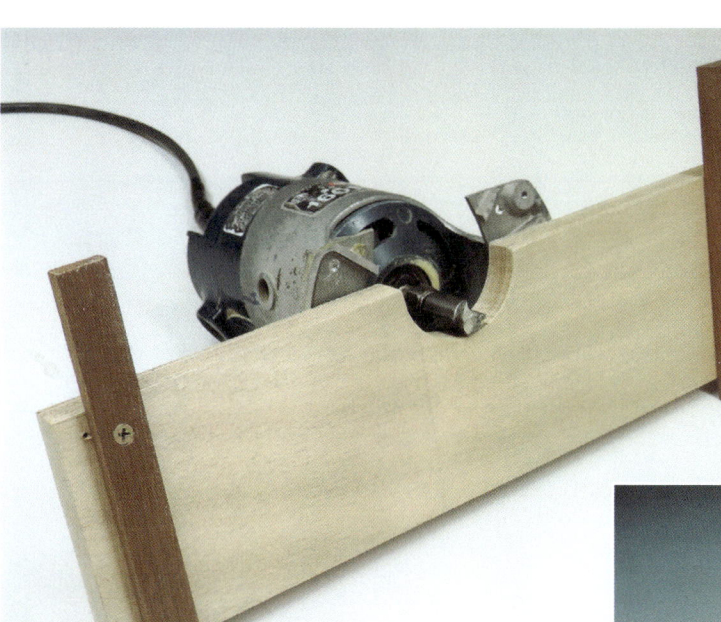

The stops (sticks screwed to the outer edges) should be positioned to keep the router bit from biting the ramps.

The stops need to be cut short on the aft ends (as shown on left) to keep from catching the clamps used to hold the stock in place.

Yes, our router base was heavily modified for a different task. Not necessary...

The router bit we are using is called a straight plunge bit. It needs to be sharp.

If the tips of your ramps are about 1/8" thick, **set your router bit a little deeper** than that.

The scarfs need to be rough-cut first, either on a bandsaw or with a power planer. Place the stock in the jig to mark for cutting. **The stock should be straight**, but if it's not, try to arrange the scarfs so that when the stock is clamped in the jig, the tip lays flat.
Running stock through a thickness planer before cutting scarfs will help straighten and flatten.

The surface of the rough-cut scarf should be below the level of the ramps (can be much more of a gap below the sled than what's shown below).

Carefully center the stock in the jig before clamping as close to the scarf as the sled will allow. Use 2 clamps. If the tip of the rough-cut scarf is not laying flat to the jig, see next page.

The stock shown being scarfed is only 5" wide. We moved the stops on the sled inboard to cut as shown.

Because of the bit rotation, all 4 edges of the scarf should be cut in the **clockwise** direction (as shown) to avoid splintering.

Hold the router low on the base to keep the sled flat to the ramps, but **don't let your fingers wander into the danger zone.**

After cutting all four edges, continue "boxing the field" until there is nothing left to cut.

Photo on right shows a scarf that needed to be re-cut because one edge of the tip lifted slightly and made an end that was not square (as can be seen).

We clamped the lifting edge flat (after centering and clamping the stock) and applied a small bead of hot-melt glue to the edge and allowed the glue to fully cool before removing the clamp(s).

The router bit won't be damaged by the glue and the remaining glue can be cut away with a sharp chisel.

The resulting scarfs should be square at both ends and should be the same length.
Assemble the scarf on a flat surface (next page) to check the fit.

The beauty of a scarfing jig is that if the jig is accurate and the stock is flat, the scarfs should fit well without having to fuss with them. **Both ends of the scarf should match (photo on right) and both sides of the scarf (below) should look the same** when the scarf is laid out flat. If adjustment is needed, use a sharp block plane or a stiff & flat sanding block.

A flat surface is needed to glue the scarf on. A piece of lumber that is flat and straight (and a bit wider) is perfect as it can be blocked up off the bench (or laid on sawhorses) for clamping the scarfs (below).

Running a board like this through a thickness planer will remove any cupping and help make it straighter.

To keep the parts straight edgeways when gluing, clamp something long and straight to one edge of the board.

The longer and straighter this piece is (let's call it a stop), the easier it will be to line the parts up when gluing.

With the parts straight and flat, slide them toward or away from each other until the best fit is achieved and then mark the exposed edge as shown.

Make sure that the parts are not trying to climb over each other.

A fatter glue line in part of the joint is better than forcing a joint to fit by squashing it together with clamps.

In fact, we only clamp at the ends of the joint as shown below, but we use another flat board over the top of the joint as a "press". This can be a piece of framing lumber that has been run through the planer to flatten and straighten it. It should be about 3 times the length of the scarf and a bit narrower if possible.

Gluing (please see notes on page 16 & 37) starts with a thorough priming with un-thickened epoxy. We use a short section of roller and a palette to apply the epoxy as the roller is faster, less messy, and cheaper than using a brush. Note the plastic sheet ready for gluing.

Apply more un-thickened epoxy after letting the first coat soak in for a bit.
Thicken a small amount of epoxy to about catsup consistency and apply with the fine teeth of a notched spreader to only one of the scarf joint faces.
Use the spreader at a flat angle to apply less epoxy.

Plastic sheet should be applied as shown before placing the parts.

Push the parts tight against the stop and line up the alignment marks (just visible below) before applying **another layer of plastic and the "press".** Clamp at the ends of the press as shown.

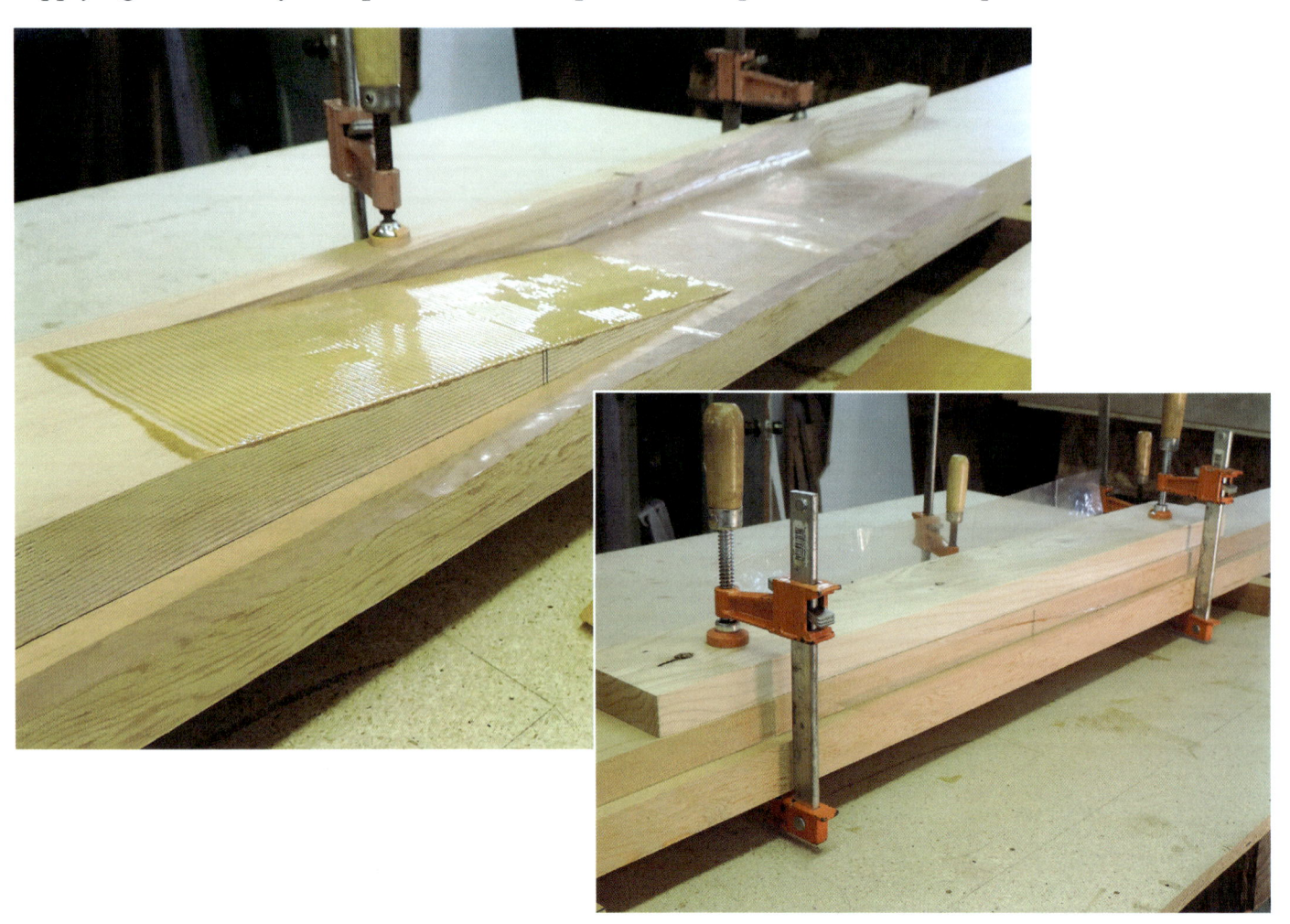

Check again that the parts are tight to the stop and that the alignment marks are lined up before placing clamps at either end of the scarf as shown.

NOTES ON SURFACE PREP, TEMP, AND GLUING.

For highly loaded scarf joints (such as those in spars), the router cut scarf surfaces should be block sanded with a flat plywood block with sharp, fine, sandpaper stuck to it.

After sanding, switch to sharper paper and sand again.

The attempt is to open the cells of the wood to better absorb epoxy. A scarf joint surface cut with a very sharp block plane may be the best for penetration of epoxy.

The temperature of the wood when gluing effects epoxy penetration drastically. The ideal is to have the wood warm, but stable or cooling as the gluing process happens. This encourages more penetration of the un-thickened epoxy before adding thickened epoxy and clamping. Gluing when the temperature of the wood is increasing is to be avoided.

The choice of fillers for thickening epoxy for gluing scarfs is important.
406 Colloidal silica inhibits penetration, which is good because after the joint is clamped, penetration is not wanted. 2/3rds (or so) of the filler added should be colloidal silica.
403 Microfiber Filler or 404 High Density Filler should be added (in lesser quantities) to further strengthen the epoxy. **The microfiber filler is coarser**. This will help keep all the glue from being squeezed out of the joint if over-clamping should occur.
Allow epoxy to cure hard before moving scarfed parts.

ADDENDUM: FILLING HOLES WITH A SYRINGE (a page from <u>EPOXY BASICS</u>)

Some people try to avoid drilling lots of holes when building a boat. We drill as many holes as we need to and don't worry about it at all, because filling holes with epoxy in a syringe is so easy.

Unlike a putty knife, filling holes with a syringe fills the holes all the way, (no coming back later after sanding to fill again). Most importantly, the mounds left by the syringe are a fraction of the effort to remove (with a sanding block) compared to the smears left by a putty knife.

To **color match** (for bright finishes), try mixing colloidal silica with a little 410 Microlight Fairing Filler. To this add a pinch of low density filler to darken for a color much like Okoume plywood.
Force thickened epoxy into the syringe with the stir stick.

Syringe the epoxy into the holes.

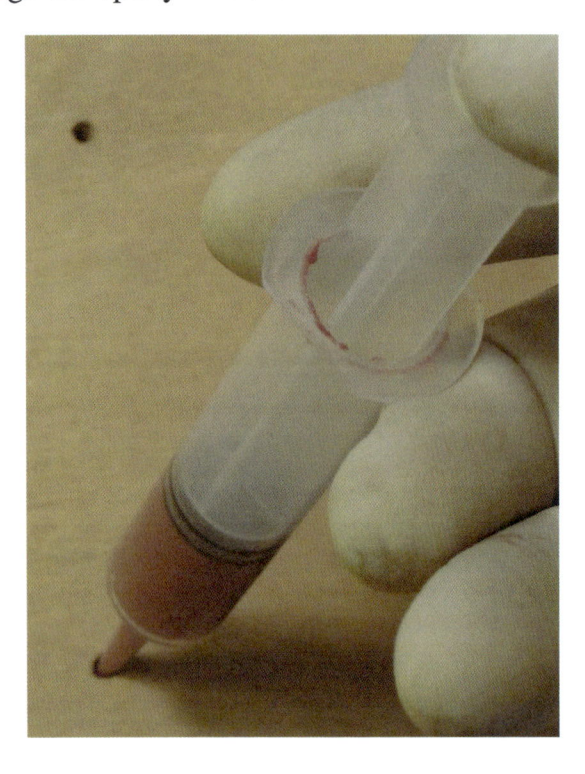

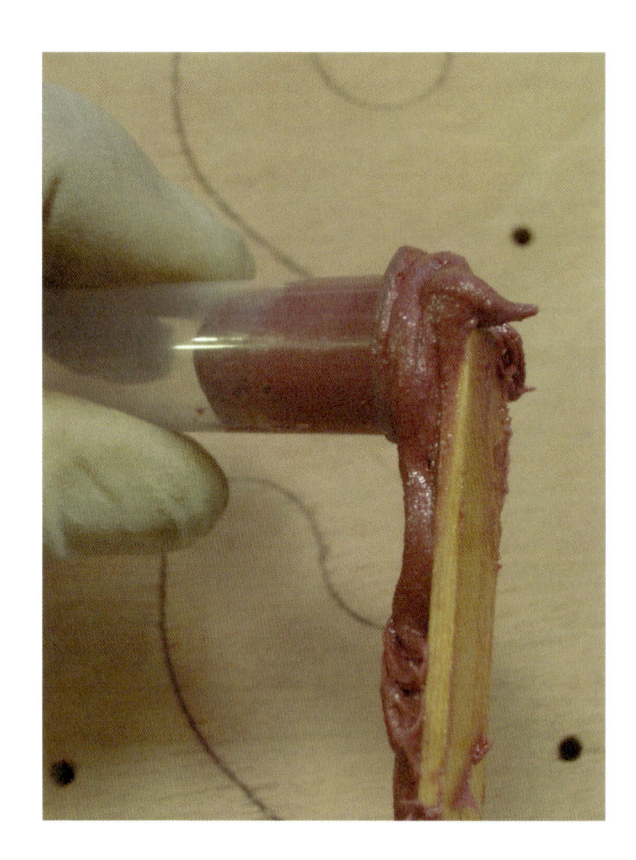

Leave a mound of epoxy over the hole.

To get multiple uses of a syringe, leave a tiny bit of epoxy in the syringe when finished, after this cures hard, cut a small amount of the tip off, flex the tip and pull the plunger out.

If the rubber part has epoxy stuck to it, remove it and bash it with a hammer, then pick off the epoxy.

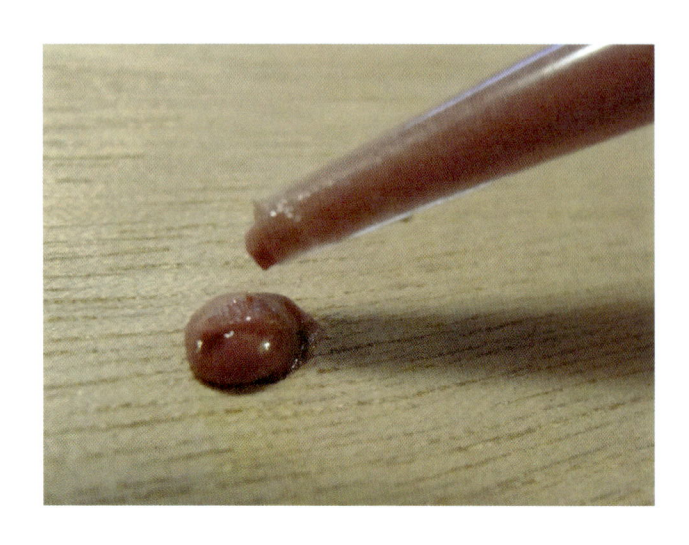

Printed in Great Britain
by Amazon